The Coloring Book

Because life isn't so black & white
and our experiences color
who we are

ISAIAH FRIZZELLE

A Day 8 LLC Book

Day8

Day 8 LLC
www.isaiahfrizzelle.com

Ordering Information:
For details, contact day8llc@gmail.com

Print ISBN: 978-0-578-98719-4

Neither author nor publisher is engaged in rendering professional advice or services to the individual reader. The ideas, procedures, and suggestions in this book are not intended as a substitute for consulting with your physician in regards to your health. Neither the author nor publisher shall be liable or responsible for any loss or damage allegedly arising from any information or suggestion in this book.

Printed in the United States of America on SFI Certified paper.

First Edition
Illustrated by Isaiah Frizzelle

To the little kid in me (you), thank you for continuing to show up;

Blue Print

"Priming"

WE'RE STARTING NEW

Imagine your life as a coloring book.

You don't need to be an artist to appreciate art. You likely enjoy music, movies, paintings, or photography. The mediums differ, but they all have something in common; Art begins with a clean slate. layers are added to create an awesome, abstract, unique, visceral piece. As an artist, I can promise you there are A TON of frustrating moments during the creation process. There are moments of doubt, vulnerability, fear, defeat, anger, happiness, elation, and personal experiences that influence the creations altogether.

By the way, I'm not asking you to be an artist right now (some of you probably sighed in relief), I'm simply having you look at something objectively.

Throughout this book we are going to think of this "coloring book" as an extension of us. By the end of this book I promise that you will have a more abstract and respected view of yourself, others, and the experiences that make people not so "Black & White". If you're willing to go on this journey you will understand and appreciate that you are your finest work of art as well as the creator, curator, and critic.

I mistakenly considered myself a pretty "vanilla" person with a lack of "highlights". I cook, I exercise, I create things, I bake (one of my favorites), there's a bunch I do. I love books, long walks and quiet time. All of these things make me who I am, but I didn't think there was much interesting about me. Sound familiar ? Me, myself, & I talk-a lot! We multitask

which means there isn't always time to listen. We just focus on getting things done and moving on to the next task, but here's a wealth of knowledge in your experiences. you and I are FAR from uninteresting, you just have to have a willingness to acknowledge your "color palette".

You can downplay an experience that left a major imprint on how you function today. You could have a hidden talent or quirk that may be something much more profound. But we were told to paint with colors that would appease others. Most of us stopped looking at the things we did as worthwhile because we undervalued our own interests. Every canvas starts blank, and then there are additions made to paint the whole picture.

If you haven't given yourself the support emotionally, mentally, physically, artistically, ... are you willing to be that peace for yourself now ? You can be completely honest and say no if that's what you feel, but understand this, the person holding you from your "peace" now is not the same person that discouraged you previously. Color on your life with anything that appeals to you.

The Work

PAPER TRAIL

Have fun, it's your first coloring page.

Throughout reading this book, keep it close by and whenever those "icky" thoughts creep up, give yourself a moment, take a look at that page and with some grace and patience say " We are starting something new, now".

* Any blank page in this book are yours. Look at it before you move to the next chapter, write on it, but let it be a an opportunity for a "clean slate".

PACK YOUR BAGS, BABY WE ARE GOING ON A JOURNEY!! ...And grab some snacks!!

"I'm perfectly Im-perfect"

Let's face it, society has primed us to look for meaning in our possessions and professions, and in turn we lose ourselves trying.

It's impossible to have this complete immunity from competing or feeling less than your peers when it seems they're progressing a lot faster than you in whatever they're pursuing (and forget if it's the same field as you).

It eats us up, but the truth is, it's not their success that bothers us, it's our lack of "success" and even more our fear of our own "incompetence".

At one point or another your parents have probably said to you, "why can't you be like so and so" or "wow, their parents must be proud".

"OH that's cool I'll sit right here and eat my food and hope my chewing drowns you out".

It stings, and while it's just words to them, (sometimes) they've planted a seed of fungus in the most delicate part of our being that will continue to grow and fester.

The truth is, we never feel good enough, we don't know how. Yes there are some people who are content with where they are and what they have; That's great if it's a healthy contentment but the majority are forever searching even if they're successful by societal definition.

The worst is when you have a set-back in pursuit of your goals and you're not where you think you should be at your age.

It's a silent killer.

You feel "off". If I could depict it as a mental image I'd say for me it feels like the entire town wanting nothing to do with me because I have that "unsuccessful" disease. A little dramatic but it feels like being an outcast and the world is moving along without you, and as hard as you try to keep pace and catch up, the inevitable is that you'll get left behind.

Hopefully you're not hiding under a table by this point, because here's the flip side, even though your circumstances are not perfect, it does not mean you're not perfect in those circumstances.

It's a Yoda thing to throw out there, but what if you can hold onto that concept and believe it?

As I write this I'm at one of the lowest points I've experienced - and there have been many- but this would probably be one in the hall of fame.

No matter what I've worked on, attempted, wished, prayed for, my current circumstances still make me feel as if I'm inevitably coming up short and that I'm a defect.

folks I know are married, have kids, are advancing in their careers and from my standpoint it's as if I haven't budged. Is it true ?

NOT AT ALL.

Interestingly enough while I write this, there's this little annoying and very persistent voice that reminds me "it's not over yet, we'll be fine".

No matter how frustrated, down trotted, and broken I may feel, that little invisible voice I hold onto is still in my grasp.

why?

I don't know.

Because deep down, past the dark place that exists in me and my head there's that reality of who I am and what I'm meant to be.

It fights endlessly (must be on roids).

I guess it's beyond hope because hope (to me) is the wishing of change without working towards it.

I remind myself that I deserve the things I seek.

I've worked for them, I continue to work for them.

I've sacrificed for them.

And the things that happen to me that aren't so good don't imply I'm not "good".

If you knew how many times I've had to remind myself of that on the regular. If you knew how tough it is to even believe it some days...I mean you're probably well aware, because there's no new news or revelation I'm writing. My experiences are not unique, but how I choose to deal with them can be. Sometimes our best defense is to show up. Show up for yourself and be a pain in the ass about it so your insecurities say "Looks like they aren't letting up and we are running out of steam".

That's it, do one thing that is intentionally toward that goal. Don't have grand expectations, just recognize you've made an effort and if consistent, will add up and add to your journey.

Who the hell wants a perfect person ? Screw that! Recognize your flaws as the things that piece you together and make you someone worth getting to know, and because of those flaws you've made a point to just work at your "you".

That's all.

Take the critiques like water and just keep working.

Falling forward is never failing.

Perfectionism stems from self disdain. To be perfect implies that who you are is defective, and if you are working on yourself with that mindset then you will never fully embrace the person at work; Just the false belief that they (you) are not "Working hard enough".

The moment you accept that you will forever be a work in progress- and that is the best thing that life has to offer- is the moment you can fully love you.

The Work

What's something important to you that you've been working at but not quite there yet ?

 Write it down.

Make small goals to get closer; trust me it's possible, lean in.

Now I want you to write down things that come to mind in the duration of your pursuit.

Say to yourself " I'm not here to be perfect, that's not my job. That's not my life's work."

If you are determined and diligent, those small wins will add up.

"Now you're speaking my language"

SPEAKING TO YOURSELF IN A LANGUAGE THAT YOU UNDERSTAND.

You talk to yourself a lot.

You're doing it right now (you're probably laughing because you know you are).

But did you know there is a language you speak, and a language your mind, body, and soul understands ?

Hold on to your hats as I break this down.

I was talking to a friend recently and our conversations always lead to some kind of self discovery and I LOVE THAT. He was telling me that he gets more accomplished when he writes.

"It's my vessel, I feel like I get more accomplished when I actually write things down."

You hear all the time to make a list and check it off. For some, it can just be a practical thing of checks and balances, for others there's a deeper meaning.

I write a lot (hence this creation you're reading). When I'm upset, I write, when I'm sad, I write. I write 5 gratitudes a night. When I want to remind my friends or someone special how much they mean to me, I make sure it's something they can go back and read.

Writing is the language my mind, emotions, and productivity respond to the most.

I didn't realize how much of a necessity it was for me, but it was something I'd do when I was younger... I was a young poet. Some auditions required me to rap, so I'd write my own verses, not out of pretension, but I enjoyed finding ways to put my thoughts into a piece of work, and if it had a flow, FORGET IT I was unstoppable!!

I don't always think I'm the most verbally expressive person, but the truth is I much rather write things down and just let it flow.

Some days I feel stifled and it's a chore for me to sit down and write; not because I don't want to (because I do enjoy it) it's the mental production I work it up to be beforehand. In my head it's like I'm going to the guillotine when I plan to sit down and write, in reality my mind couldn't be more at peace.

Where there is little resistance, there is the most promise.

When you find yourself hitting walls with other things you distract yourself with, it can be because you're forcing your body to speak a language it doesn't understand and never learned.

When you find that you're drained or frustrated and pent up with a bunch of "stuff" , pay attention to that. You're not giving your body what it needs.

Pay attention to the things that give you peace or you find yourself acclimated to do. I'm not talking about sitting on the couch and binge watching tv while stuffing your face, or scrolling on social media for hours, I'm talking about those things that you don't think much of but enjoy or just feel accomplished after doing.

Be more aware of what people around you gravitate to you for.

Some folks are amazing builders. Other people may be exceptionally crafty, Some are great planners, cooks, artists, writers, and there are a bunch of outlets you may have not been plugging into (see what I did there?) out of lack of attention or sheer doubt of your skills.

Don't wait for someone else to tell you you're good enough to do what feels good to you.

Once you start paying attention to what your body craves, it will be much easier.

Since we are on the topic of self talk...

How do you actually talk to yourself ?

You locked yourself out.

You lose your wallet.

You forgot that "thing".

You overshared ...

You "cared too much".

You got your heart broken.

That date didn't go as planned.

You didn't get that job.

you couldn't do the thing that your kid asked of you.

You didn't live up to someone else's "should" in terms of your life.

What kind of "fuck up" or "idiot" did you call yourself ?

It's all good to admit that you said something pretty rude to yourself in those moments, but I have to warn you, after you admit to it, you're now aware of your self-talk and now that means you will actively work at changing it. You deserve it. That's not up for debate.

My acting teacher used to say to us " don't say anything to yourself that you wouldn't say to a three year old.", and while some people are capable of being pretty reckless (which is also a major indication of their past), the average person would not look a three year old in the face and tell them that they are a failure in any capacity. The same applies here.

To yourself

Regardless of how old you are at this very moment, there's still the child in you looking for approval, validation, acceptance, safety, and love. We get older but there are still parts of us that never "grew up", they just had to get older.

Accidents, moments of mishaps, mistakes, and carelessness all exist. We are human. You get nervous or you get angry, you give yourself the third degree for it.

Where did you learn it from ? We are not instinctively self deprecating, that's a nurture thing.

Somewhere along the lines someone said some pretty harsh things to you if you didn't do something "properly", and when they left you in charge of yourself, you continued to carry out the punishment.

Sticks and stones may break my bones but words will emotionally leave some wounds that never properly heal...

I think that was the real nursery rhyme.

Words are so damaging to your core without you realizing it.

Your parents may have said some hurtful things to you growing up, trust me they say it to themselves too because someone else said it to them.

But we have to be the kind of parent to ourselves that we needed when we were younger.

I know there are times we jokingly say things like " I'm such a goofball", or "I'm a total spaz". You may not realize it in the moment, but you are framing your inner little self to believe those things and identify with them.
Sometimes we are the monsters that were under our beds and in our closets as children.

What I mean by that is, when no one is looking, our inner critic haunts us with all the things we strongly dislike about ourselves.
So here's my challenge to you: Say some kind things to yourself.

It sounds so cheesy but if you heard someone calling another person the same things you call yourself, would you be okay with that (I hope not)?!

How does it feel when someone says nice things to you like, "Hey I'm proud of you!""good job!" "you're a great person and I'm glad to know you." How about saying those things to yourself ? If someone says those things to you, are you able to receive and believe them ? If not, start there.

You won't believe them at first so don't worry. It took time and persistence to believe all those negative things about yourself so don't give up.

Your inner you is a sponge and will absorb whatever it is given. It doesn't know the difference. Your job is to make conscientious work of telling yourself all the good things you value about you. What are you good at ? Again what do people say to you ?

But promise me. From this moment on YOU WILL MAKE AN ACTIVE EFFORT TO BE KINDER TO YOURSELF. How you treat yourself is how you think and treat others.

The Work

For the next week:

I want you to do something for me and for you. I want you to take a minute, and write down some things that you like about yourself. Doesn't have to be a long list for now, this is just to get the process going.

When things don't seem to be going your way or maybe you make a mistake, before you say one foul thing to yourself, take a minute and say " I will do better. This is just a moment, not a monument. "

Say some kind things to yourself in the mirror. Say them in your head ! If you notice a difference, what is it ?

Gray Area

" I'm starving , let's eat ! "

THE EGO

Your ego is bats*&% crazy and probably has a tapeworm mmk?
There I said it.

When a baby is hungry it wails- I mean adults do it too- but your ego is
a little more manipulative and gluttonous than a baby (Apparently I ate
a lot growing up but I digress).

Before a child is conceived, people are already parenting "ego babies"
(themselves) in their relationships.

As you read on, I want you to keep your ego in mind.

RELATIONSHIP

It's something I've noticed in all relationships, not just romantic. It's a waltz that revolves around the lack/need of attention. The dating culture has made it almost a game of having the upper hand in the situation; "I don't owe anyone, but they should really recognize that I'm a catch... and the only way they can understand that is if I limit my access and engagement... you know, play it cool."

To be brief, dating is a very vulnerable space. Some show up for fun, others show up for further investment, but that does not negate the reality that it's a nerve-wracking place to be. And when exchanges take place, it's important to recognize the ego at work. It desires acknowledgment and that's it.
Example:

Let's use someone who is already in a committed relationship. There has been a lack of one person feeling valued... in some scenarios, someone comes along who seems to be more interested in one person than their significant other has been showing. Morally, it's apparent something is awry, but the ego just punched out for lunch and is ready to munch (I laughed reading that and I'm not sorry).

Entertaining attention from someone else, to get the attention of someone else, who you feel is not giving you the attention that you desire; ego.

"My needs are not being met and I'm hurting" = "I want them to hurt". I'm sure you can think of a few things you've done or considered to get someone's attention-yeaaaa that thing, that's your ego.

Your ego, if not properly addressed and maintained, will eat anything in sight, and never be satiated. When it's finished you will be left to clean up, and some stains are impossible to get out.

See what I mean about the ego ? It doesn't care so much about who is consumed in the process, it just wants to eat. The truth is that our egos are scared and fragile, but the more we remind ourselves that we are ok, that our existence is not diminished by minor actions, we can prevent ourselves from acting out of ego. It takes work and gusto to call yourself out, but the next time something really makes you want to retaliate in such a way that gains you attention and makes someone else feel negatively, recognize "that's my ego".

The Work

Your work is to just be mindful. Moment to moment being aware of when your ego creeps up in situations where you feel small or inadequate. Before acting on impulse say to yourself "This is my ego, so what do I actually need right now ? "

Sometimes it's a need to feel seen, heard, valued... it all comes down to feeling loved. So be brave, ask yourself "is this what I need ?" and if so that's okay, we all do.

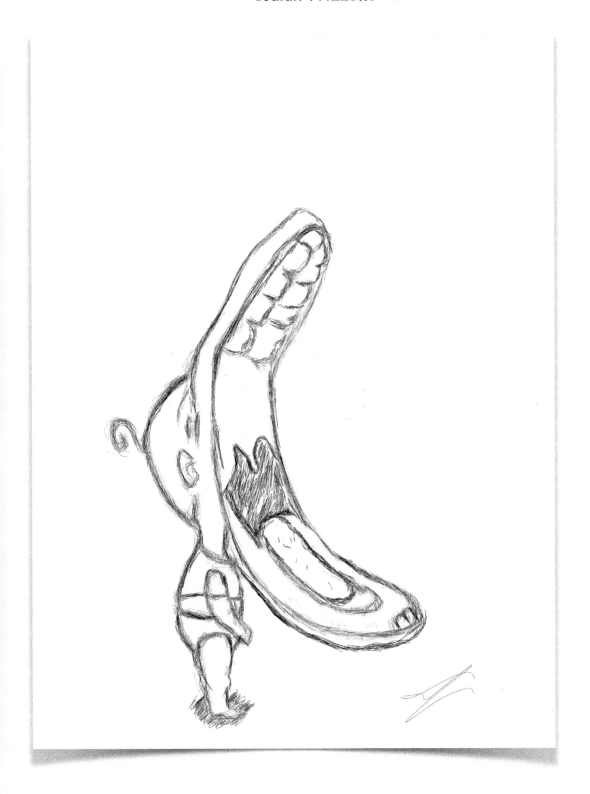

"EVERYTHING IS FIIIINEEEE"

That right there ... you've said it before. Stop it.

You're giving mixed signals. Not so much to who you're saying it to, but to yourself. My usual go-to is, "it's all good." but, plot twist, it's not.

In order to put out a fire, you need the exact location, not a "maybe" spot.

Same with emotions.

When you're unclear about how you truly feel and you're not clear about expressing it (of course in a healthy manner) then you're giving mixed directions to the place that needs attention. You're also devaluing your feelings about a situation... It's almost self-gaslighting.

"Isaiah, I can't gaslight myself ya silly rabbit" the hell you can't !!

Ever hear someone say " I don't know how I feel ?"

Honestly it's become the more common and acceptable feeling after anger, and apathy. Anger seems to be conditional as well; There's a time and place for it.

This is all a round about way of saying that over time apathy replaces all the emotions you were never allowed to truly feel or express.

Granted, gaslighting is a learned behavior, but eventually we learn to devalue our process, and also give way to tolerating more things that we probably shouldn't.

I think it's safe to say that a large population of men (not all guys) were not allowed to express feelings growing up.
"Toughen up", " You're so sensitive", " Stop crying like a little girl",
" You better not cry"...

There's a resilience that comes with that, yes, but there's also some blocked reservoirs that find other ways to empty out.

And it's not just guys, I've realized women have been victims to it as well.

I was taping an audition recently. The content was all there. The character clearly had some depth to work with and some things to work through.

MEAAAN WHILE I danced around those waters the entire time. Maybe I dipped a toe in but that was as far as I would go; Swimming was prohibited.

Honestly, It frustrated me because the inner dialogue of " why can't you just open up? " creeped into my mind the entire time. Completely disregarding I had minutes, days, months, and years of experience building emotional walls.

I was capable, but my emotions would creep to the surface at the weirdest times, ESPECIALLY when I didn't want them to.

I walked away from that audition saying to myself " when exactly will you give yourself permission?"

Could be performance anxiety but that's not all of it, not by a long shot.

There's a damn panic room I've built in my own mind and heart that refuses to allow "the feels".

We were born with feelings, it's survival, it's social cues, it's necessary to properly navigate any and every situation when dealing with yourself or someone else; So what exactly is the problem?

Society says it's not okay to show anything other than happy... Until they're ready. we're all a bunch of children that were forced to grow up, never truly fixing the things that were necessary to fix back then.

Interestingly enough we find relationships that reflect what we need to work on.

we find relationships that reinforce a certain behavior, or lack thereof. We do everything but address what's necessary to be better. *see substance (of any kind including food and physical intimacy) abuse*

Get comfortable with saying things like "This makes me uncomfortable", or "that hurt my feelings". Trust me, it's still my work BUT what I've learned is no one who truly cares about your well-being wants to know they are responsible for you not feeling okay.

Let's make this clear, your feelings are valid. Your feelings do not need permission from someone else to exist and be given attention.

Experiences can give us a false sense of responsibility when it comes to the people that have wronged us. We rationalize the need to take care of their feelings by protecting them from the hurt that they have caused.

"Everything is fine" comes from not wanting to upset anyone with your existence.

Not knowing how you actually feel comes from suppressing how you actually feel constantly. TAKE UP SPACE!

If you fear abandonment, you probably have a major issue with expressing yourself out of losing people for being "too much".

The Work

Simple in text but a little more brave to practice.

Next time a situation affects you, don't say, "it's all good" don't say "everything is fine" take up space and let your existence be felt, just by saying how you feel.

Of course in the most constructive way possible.

"Hey I feel/ This made me feel... "

"So you want revenge"

One day you wake up, start your day with your morning routine

(mantra, coffee, workout, music) and mentally prepare yourself for what's ahead. Could be some good stuff, could be some teeth pulling obligations, but in all, there are things you need to tackle, because it's a new day!

Then you get a notification and your stomach sinks. A blast from the past... That "thing" that you've worked hard to get over or still currently working through comes ringing, in all its glory.

Not too long ago I walked away from a taxing and toxic situation. It sounds hokey, but usually from the moment I meet someone I can tell what kind of soul I'm working with, but I also have fumbled forward through the concept that the people we meet have something significant to add to our lives.

In the thick of things it's hard to see the silver lining of a situation and you're blinded with frustration, but time passes.

Time passed for me... 7 months to be exact. I was waking up to start my day and my phone buzzed. It was a message from an old acquaintance about the person (let's call him Meyers because I like horror movies) I had a falling out with. The very things I suspected had been happening were confirmed. The entire time I'm listening I felt uneasy.

We feel horrible in those situations where the perpetrator is being praised while you are trying to maintain your reputation and character. The initial response is to fight back, get to the world before they do, but what does that do ? The thing about stories is they have to be sustained, and if your character - which is a consistent display of who you are at your core - contradicts the narrative then you will outlast whatever fallacy that comes against you. Meyers would find a way to justify his behavior and look past mine but he's developed a pattern where his actions have been imprinted on others... and so have mine. Despite anything, our character has been put on display.

The best revenge is no revenge at all...

Although in the moment of pain and confusion that's THE LAST THING you want to hear. "Screw being the bigger person this fucker did some hurtful things and I want reparations."

Can we talk for a second though ? ... Just you, me, and your pain...

You're hurt, and some things you are probably still recovering from and that's all good. You are allowed to be and feel everything in this moment, but listen to me, I promise you the best revenge is to go through all of that and come out better. It may not make sense right now, It's moment to moment work when you have to relive something that deeply affected you. It will not change overnight, but don't invite who you are not into your life to represent who you truly are. Yes we are all capable of some pretty sinister things, but it's the follow through that matters. It may not always feel great, but you will always be taken care of AND I AM A TESTAMENT OF THAT. I've been in a better place completely. New people, opportunities, outlook, all because of what I experienced with one person. Your blessing isn't always beautifully wrapped up, it can be a hot mess.

Hurt people, hurt people. Healing people recognize that they are working through enough to know who they are becoming is worth more than an "eye for an eye" moment.

Your eyes are set on being better. Keep that focus.

The work

Think about the moment of a missed opportunity for vindication:

Get a black pencil or crayon. Draw a box. Inside that box write the person's name.

Now take a different color, your favorite color and draw a larger box around the black one.

Write your accomplishments since the incident in the space; could be new friends, relationship, opportunities, feelings, books, etc. Anything that has been an asset to you since then.

Now I want you to write your name at the top of the box.

You embody this box.

You and your accomplishments are so much larger and take up more space in your life than the incident. We recognize and acknowledge the incident since we have valid feelings that exist because of it, but that was a necessary evil for us to be who we are now. This is revenge. The best kind.

"The Art of Betrayal"

"911 WHATS YOUR EMERGENCY ?" "UM YEA MY TRUST WENT MISSING. I LEFT IT WITH SOMEONE AND NOW THEY NO LONGER HAVE IT."

Let's say it together, BETRAYAL is a bitch!

Now exhale.

The truth: Betrayal is probably one of the best things to happen to you in a weird, fucked up kind of way; but only IF you're truly willing to trust the process. I'm talking about all that hurt, anger, embarrassment, guilt and loneliness that comes with it.

Basically betrayal is a soccer mom(or dad) with a minivan full of emotions and as they all run like hell from the van, each of them carries something very important in their bags.

And the award for best metaphor goes to!

You will learn so much about yourself and someone else in how they be-treat you.

There's levels to this:

Betrayal is about self; Yourself and themselves.

It's not always a literal backstab although those things can happen also.

I personally feel like the worst betrayal is the subtle form, the one that sneaks up on you.

To travel deeper, what about an abusive relationship, emotional, mental, or physical. You've trusted this person wouldn't hurt you but they did. That's betrayal. They've capitalized on your trust in them.

But understand we are more than capable and can be more than responsible for betraying ourselves.

To be or not to betray yourself

When it comes to relationships,(friends and family), you may have confided in one or the other with something that affected you deeply.

There is a moment of difference, and the very thing you trusted them with they've loaded their bow with. Bulls eye. Or the secret finds an opening during one of their conversations and it's out!

What do you do? What did I do?

Shit, I got quiet duh Haha!

Sometimes I got quiet, other times I broke down in their face, waited until I was alone, or just pushed it down altogether.

When your emotions are flaring and when you're exposed I don't think you're witty enough to have a comeback.
I'll admit, sometimes in that moment I wanted to hurt back and I may have, but in the cases that come to mind, each individual reminded me that "Trust expires the moment it's content is exposed to air."

Shock and confusion are indeed the initial reactions, " I can't believe they said that", " I'm embarrassed", "Try not to let it show", "fight back" "brush it off"...

By this point my face or yours is running hot, your breaths might be a little shorter, you feel something in your chest, and boy does my stomach hurt.

It's literally a code red for your body. You're wounded. You're not gushing blood (depending on the situation), no broken bones, or anything physically evident to indicate to this person that they just now cut you deep.

Maybe your mind is clouded and blank all at once. At the moment the only thing that comes to mind is " I can't trust them either". Just like that. Mentally it's like turning off the light in a room (relationship) and walking out closing the door behind never to return to the room again. The people may still exist in your life, but the same level of love and trust has probably dwindled tremendously.

I had to look at a pattern of mine where it appeared I was always on the shitty end of people doing me wrong (major or minor) And understanding and accepting that the common denominator in all of it ...ME.

"you're the common denominator in all of the situations", Whether it's you taking things too personal or just cultivating situation-ships that lend themselves to an unpleasant outcome;

"You give too easily"

"You care"

And you fail to realize others don't at all or just as much as you do. When it comes down to it it's neither person's fault, or is it ?

"Have no expectations" is a phrase people use but in reality no one really is capable of in interpersonal relationships. Even selfish people have expectations of getting their needs met. You will always have expectations when it comes to something that matters to you. When you're not genuinely invested, you won't ... because there's nothing for you to gain. When you give a part of yourself, maybe you don't expect the same back but you do expect one thing; being able to trust that other person or situation (job, home, partnership) with whatever piece of you they have. Friendship, relationship, partnership, it doesn't matter because as humans our need to connect is vital and our survival relies on it.

Sometimes we just simply betray ourselves.

What are your expectations ? Be completely honest with yourself so you have a clear idea.

We kick ourselves for trusting people but how else do you build trust than to attempt to establish it with someone?

When we trust someone or someone trusts us with safety in any capacity and we do something repeatedly to discredit that, we are betraying or being betrayed.

Here's the truth, People don't "change" as ideally as we hope. We are creatures of habit and change takes work. Who you are, and where you fall on either side of that is who you will be. It's a reality to wrap your head around. If you constantly find yourself in situations that leave you feeling taken advantage of, or lopsided then it's your habits that you've decided not to change for one reason or another.

Our needs in those moments are not being met and it has nothing to do with that person. There's history to the pattern and it stems from a much deeper vein of disappointment. At some point in time we are taught certain behaviors, we're taught certain hurts, any new people or situations that remind us of those feelings is simply a window into a past of messy moments.

You can only be betrayed by someone that has your trust, Not necessarily earned it, but nonetheless has it.

But, here's the piece, we exist in a world where people practice opposite of what they preach.

THEMSELVES

It's easy to tell someone that their feelings are not valid or their reaction to a situation that hurt them is over the top. But it's easy

when it's not happening to you.

We value our own feelings, space, perception, and experiences much more than someone else's because their emotes don't rest on us naturally; We can't feel what they feel. Lacking empathy is trendy...
People want you to get over what they've done to you faster than they're willing to hold themselves accountable.
"Get over it" is popular.

People project their past onto you; things they haven't let go of and when you're affected by it they say "get over it " all while their offense is because of them still holding onto their stuff - you know because their pain is justified, yours is not.

I know personally how important it is to not betray someone to the best of my ability because I've been betrayed.

Someone else could care less about betraying someone because at one point in time they were betrayed; doesn't matter if that person (you) was involved, that just becomes their justification.

Betrayal makes us feel weird, and by weird I mean exposed, defenseless, silly, weak, and in some way we think that we deserve to be betrayed, we were responsible for being let down.

STOP THAT.

A betrayal towards you is not a reflection of you.

You did not ask for this person to do that.

Any moment you are sincerely vulnerable should not be an invite for you to ridicule yourself for it.

It's important to stop subconsciously betraying ourselves when we are in a moment of pain.

Discernment goes a long way. If things don't feel right, trust that. If someone feels "off" to you for one reason or another, lean into that a little. We are animals and we have instincts. I'm not suggesting you go into every situation with the expectation to be exposed, I'm saying when your senses perk up a little, understand why.

That is a major step in avoiding situations that can potentially lead to disappointment.

Notice I didn't say never trust again. If you want to be trusted, and are trustworthy, then be willing to extend it.

The Work

Don't betray yourself anymore. How do you do that?

First, you have to start with small to do lists, that involve you completing work... You need to know that you can trust yourself and do what you say you will .

Practice discernment. Ask yourself why you may be sharing this information with this other person. What are the qualities that they have that appeal to you and why?

Are you looking for acceptance? Approval?

Validation?

Connection?

How does your gut feel when you think about the thing you want to share?

Have they shown you that they can in fact be trustworthy ?

If it's a relationship you're truly trying to fertilize, start small. Plant small seeds.

Never be in a rush or feel rushed to share the tender parts of you that still require healing.

And lastly if they turn out to not be all that trusting, be able to trust yourself that you won't beat down on you so hard about their actions.

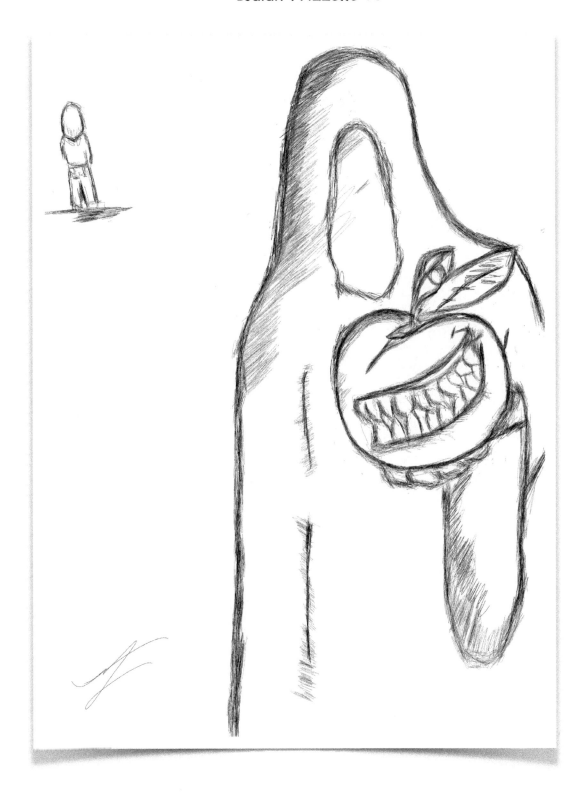

"The Art of an Apology"

"SORRY FOR YOUR INCONVENIENCE BUT WE ARE UNABLE TO TRACK YOUR APOLOGY YOU ORDERED ... WOULD YOU LIKE TO MOVE ON OR CONTINUE TO WAIT FOR DELIVERY? "

In the previous chapter we talked about the hit of a betrayal, but I'm sure you've been in a situation or even heard someone say " I'm waiting for my apology " ...

You know what's funny, people die waiting, literally. They spent the rest of their days secretly watering a hurt from a situation that was a moment in time that both parties have moved on from... physically at least. It's safe to say at least one person is pressing rewind constantly and reliving that day, while the other person is pushing fast forward or has just removed the tape (I'm old school) completely.

Have you ever thought about what's really tied to that apology you're waiting to receive ? Take a wild guess...

YOUR WORTH!

You've unknowingly wrapped your entire internal world around "I'm sorry" from one or many people. The truth, I can promise you that apology will most likely not fix your feelings about the situation or the individual.

So why do we do this to ourselves?

Respect

Acknowledgement

Worth

Validation

The truth is, some situations are damaging beyond repair. You can forgive someone, yes, but that's not an indication you condone their behavior.

We all want to be acknowledged and respected. A true apology is the recognition of both.

I agree if you wrong someone you should apologize, ego aside especially if you'd want the same, but the reality is, the ideal is a rarity .

Ask yourself if you even want this person back in your company.

Ask yourself if the lack of apology is going to keep you from your day to day; For some it might.

Will it kill you (not your ego, or your pride but literally you) if it never happens ? Simplify everything. Do it. You'll feel better

Understanding a heavily delayed apology is an indication of perception of the relationship and it's priority. It also magnifies the character of the person.

This is a tough love lesson in pill form that goes down easier when you don't hold your breath.

What if someone isn't sorry ? Can you live with that ? I don't mean just breathing and functioning. I mean deep down be able to let go of whatever grudge or grievance you hold over that relationship ?

You have to be willing to accept an apology that you never receive; For you, not them. It's a different kind of apology though.

This one is sincere. It's meaningful and thought out. It comes from understanding and respect. It's coming from you !!

What we fail to realize is that the pain we continue to feel from a moment in time is in actuality us reliving that moment putting ourselves through that cycle repeatedly. So, who is really the perpetrator now?

Forgiveness is tough because we believe that when we forgive someone we let them off the hook or approve of their behavior.

Not quite.

Not at all actually. To forgive means "I'm ready to move past this moment because it doesn't serve me. It doesn't feel good. It keeps me hurt".

Some people, myself included at one point in time have identified with a circumstance that hurt us. The hurt gave us something to feel about and be tasked with and in our weird rational thinking gave us control.

There are people who literally operate from their pain and live out their days in that only to release it into the world.

It's toxic to you and others. It's torture.

But we think we have to remain angry at people that hurt us so they know that they hurt us and because we are hurt we need them to be hurt by our hurt- I hope that was a tongue twister for you so you understand how absurd it is to put yourself through the same repeatedly.

Moving forward, understand that our reasons for forgiveness is because we deserve to not have the emotional weight of the thing that happened to us.

The Work

So maybe you're asking " how do I apologize to myself ? I didn't do anything wrong."

If you are reliving a past trauma, you are in fact doing something very wrong, to yourself.

Take your time and mean every word of this: "Hey I know that situation was painful, I'm sorry we went through that. I'm going to do better and let go of this pain I've been carrying from that moment. You didn't deserve that then and you don't deserve it now. "

Just like you'd seek changed behavior from the person you're expecting an apology from, when you apologize to yourself you also have to change your behavior. When you find yourself picking "it" up, put it right back down.

Try that apology when necessary, and when you forgive, really forgive. See that person as someone who is probably hurting otherwise they wouldn't have been so equipped and capable to do the same to you. Your forgiveness does not grant them access, but it does grant you the peace you're entitled to.Forgive and forge on.

"The Art of Apology" The Sequel

I WAS WRONG, AND IT FEELS SO RIGHT.

I've never seen an "apology" on trial for murder, but people seem afraid to be caught in a dark alley with it.

"He held me hostage and I feared for my ego, I mean my life! "
If you are a parent reading this, please, please, please with sprinkles (rainbow not chocolate) make it a habit of sincerely apologizing to your children when you're wrong. I'll explain and you will probably empathize. Trust me.

Okay back to our regularly scheduled programming *Cracks Knuckles*
"I'm sorry" and "I apologize" when you really mean it, translates to
" Hey, I hold myself accountable for my actions that affected you and I want to be more cognizant moving forward to not repeat it."
Apologies involve humility and society has pruned us to be unapologetically guilt- free (not gluten free) in our pursuits through life. "If you're affected by my actions, that is your heaping plate to eat, not mine!" A true apology is organic which is why it probably tastes funny to some.

As a collective, our moral nutrition is not the best.

A true apology is changed behavior not a phrase in the moment to elude discomfort.

"I'm sorry" doesn't make you weak when you've wronged someone, it strengthens your bond with the person (if they are willing), strengthens your integrity, strengthens your reputation, strengthens your self perception and above all trust.

A true apology has a formula:

Awareness+Acknowledgment x Correction - ego = Quality

It seems so simple but it's truly not. We spoke earlier about never receiving the apology we feel we deserve, but if you have the opportunity to give an apology when it's due and MEAN IT, well my friend you just leveled up.

An effective sincere apology doesn't allow your "A**" to interject. "I'm sorry I hurt you BUT..." or "Sorry you're upset."

Nope, Nope, Nopity NOPe!

When there's a "but" or a placement of responsibility on the other person, that's a subtle form of gaslighting and manipulation. " I don't take full or any responsibility for what happened " is the subtext.

Remember my plea with the parents? Yea well there's a reason for that. If our parents never apologize to us, or did everything but acknowledge their offense, a few things happen later:

-We grow up lacking accountability and in turn run for the exit aka deflect

-We become accustomed to mistreatment and rationalize someone else's behavior towards us.

-We always apologize because we were taught that it must be something we are doing wrong and it's our responsibility to fix the issue.

In the end we engage in toxic, imbalanced relationships with ourselves and others. It's a real shit show.

Have you ever caught yourself or someone saying "sorry" for being in someone's way as they walk into a room ? Or do they continuously apologize for expressing themselves ? That's apologizing for your existence, not an offense committed.

A key point to remember though, and probably the most important is, just because you've apologized and actually meant it, does not mean that the person is obligated to forgive you or move on as if nothing happened. If you've apologized sincerely, you did your job; nothing else is any of your business. We believe that because we apologize we are entitled to re-entry, or immunity moving forward with a clean slate. We're all cause and effect creatures, and if you can understand that, you will understand that this person may still be on their own journey as are you.

Be willing to accept an apology when given. Be willing to accept an apology when given. Be WILLING to ACCEPT an APOLOGY when it is given. You want to grow right ? Growth is on the other side of that pain you're holding onto.

Saying "sorry" may feel ugly, but man does it make you beautiful...

The Work

Apologize... and mean it. Leave your ego in the car with the windows rolled up on a hot summer day. And if you're constantly apologizing for who you are, apologize to yourself for that. Try it for the next couple of days. If you are good at being apologetic in a healthy way, then keep trucking, I'm proud of you.

"Trust Fall"

I HAVE TRUST ISSUES...

So if you've heard or said, any of the following phrases, I want you to tally it up:

"I've been hurt before."

"I gave my trust, and they betrayed me."

"I feel confused."

"I don't know how I feel."

"I don't know what I want."

"I can't make a decision to save my life."

While these are all phrases that can be overused to deflect responsibility, to not be as forthcoming or honest in terms of interest (dating culture) these phrases can definitely tell you a lot about yourself. I've learned the reason I don't trust others is because at my core I don't always trust myself. A lack of trust in worth, desires, thinking, capabilities, decisions, value. "There's nothing I trust of me, so how could I possibly be trusting of someone else ?"

Does it make sense ?

You could be saying to yourself, "well, Isaiah I have been hurt by others and I have been betrayed."

Yes! Your feelings are valid, but understand you should be validating yourself beyond just those moments of hurt. So let me ask you something, If you replay the relationship in your head, and look at everything that led up to that moment of betrayal, this person showed you signs didn't they? I don't mean something grand either, I'm talking about their patterns of communication, how they treated your feelings, how you felt around them, their presence in your life, their effort. There was a lot of inconsistency and you were putting pieces together I'm sure.

But, before we throw blame, let's look at it this way, you invited that relationship with open arms. You allowed this person in your life despite the signs. You rationalized their mode of operation, and downplayed your doubts about them. All along they were being themselves, believe it or not.

Let's dig deeper.

Our foundation (or lack thereof) for trust is a very early recipe that just sticks and we continue to use that recipe because it's what we know.

I'm talking about your relationship with your care takers.
I'll use me for a moment. My father wasn't in my life, and still to this day I can say with full conviction that it hasn't been a detriment to my growth as a human per se. There's no bitter bones, but interestingly enough I've come to learn it has created a sense of absence with other people or waiting for the other shoe to drop.

Or let's say your parents are present but still lack consistent delivery of emotional nutrients. Maybe there were times you felt unloved, upset about something, and immediately it was devalued or dishonored. It got to a point where I didn't think much of what I experienced because it " wasn't that bad or a big deal" so whenever experiences would show up I'd downplay how important it may have been to me.

You could've heard a lot of , "stop complaining", "you take everything personal", "you're too sensitive". It's not personal, but in a personal relationship with personal feelings, some things are going to hurt.

In turn, there's no longer a vocal expression of thoughts or feelings. When something did upset me I continuously told myself "dude, don't be so sensitive, it's nothing personal". I learned to be quiet, but more than anything keep showing up for whatever dish I was served.

What does that do ? Well it's telling my "inner little dude" that what he feels is not important and irrational. He's invalidated. "Buck Up!"

Gaslighting is the tool used by the people that don't want to feel guilt or accountability for what they've done. "I'll make you feel guilty for feeling your feelings before you make me feel bad for what I've done, or will do to cause them."

Through life I ushered in a lot of inconsistent relationships. Relationships that were conditional, and also felt like if I put it down they wouldn't bother to pick it up. I realized it wasn't their fault or even mine. Objectively speaking, it's just a matter of circumstances that create the proper environment for other things to take place. I cultivated relationships that replicated the relationships I knew. It wasn't intentional, it's just what I knew.

I don't trust myself because I never learned how to trust in a healthy way. But where this is wreckage there is work. I've learned to trust

myself more. If something doesn't feel right I dig a little deeper; "is this a trauma response or is there really something here that doesn't sit right ? "

We don't trust the good things in life but are all too comfortable with things that we don't deserve. Having inconsistent people in your life is no fun, but if you're comfortable or used to it then you will continue to endure and invite it. The word "loyal" gets thrown around a lot, but to show unwavering loyalty to someone who you cannot trust is appropriating mistreatment. It's creating a pattern internally. It's telling you that you deserve this treatment, even if in the moment it upsets you, " it's not that big of a deal".

You are your biggest betrayer by what you accept.

Take it off of relationships externally, what about your relationship with yourself? Your day to day. You know that goal, or that thing you said you'd start or finish ?

Are your fitness goals getting dusty and pushed into the far corner of your mental closet ? Sometimes I say I'll go for a walk, and instead I'll stay home.

This book right now has taken a while to finish because I kept putting it off. I didn't trust that the content was good enough for someone to want to pick up. But by the time you read this it will have been finished... And the content, well I'm pretty damn happy with it.

While this is a "big" task, it's still something I'm doing for myself to show that I can be trusted. Once you start showing up for yourself in the small dailies, your internal trust will shift.

You will trust your worth more. You will trust your value. Your thoughts. Feelings. Emotions. capabilities.

Unhealthy relationships won't feel as comfortable in your life because you will be taking better care of your relationship with yourself.

Make sense ?

We often make the mistake of setting out into the world to find someone we can trust and who will love us ...and still have yet to do it for ourselves.

The work

As mentioned in the betrayal chapter, it's all about recognizing opportunities to learn what trust (and betrayal) looks and feels like in our relationship with ourselves first.

Make some plans... set realistic, small goals to start, I don't care what they are, just complete them!

Ex:"Today I'll go for a walk" or "walk further".

"I'll clean out that drawer today".

"I'll give them a call."

"I'll drink more water."

Try to Journal everyday for a week... see if you can stick to it.

How about 5 gratitudes .

When you follow through (because you will), pay attention to how you feel about it, and what you think of yourself when it's complete. The little moments add up and it's imperative you rebuild some trust with yourself.

"The Rabbit"

"And for our next trick ... Sorry, it seems my assistant lost the rabbit that I forgot to provide."

PHANTOM EMOTIONAL RESPONSIBILITY.

I can say with confidence most people are emotional magicians (depending on their level, there may be other adjectives used to describe them). What do I mean ? It's a dance with ourselves (and unaware parties) when dealing with our feelings. I'm talking about holding unequipped and unqualified people accountable for our emotional needs.

But don't yell at me just yet... we ourselves not always aware of what we are actually doing... that damn rabbit just keeps moving hats!

By the way, there's no actual rabbit at all, we tell ourselves there is, because it can't be us doing this to ourselves Psh!
We tell ourselves that the people we meet and invest in will fill the voids in all aspects of our lives where we didn't receive the proper nurturing; The "Phantom" as a very good friend of mine put it.

The phantom represents the elusive "fix" or validation we think is hiding out in someone else; a partnership, a significant other, a friend, an accomplishment and they have no idea they stole our happiness.

This is probably a good time to grab a snack, just saying.

Later we will talk about the patterned relationships we cultivate and why, but for now I'll say, every person you meet is not the answer to the ambiguity you've endured prior to meeting them.

Someone's responsibility in your life is not to fix a past they had no hand in, it's to be responsible for the present space they take up. That's their ONLY JOB.

But if you are your business and you are handling the interviewing process, then you would know the job positions you're looking to fill right ? Not always, and that's bad for business.

You'll notice your level of frustration with your "employees" when the job you're looking to get done (your needs being met from a past experience) seems to be left unfinished.

To give you a clear example: Do you ever get upset with someone because they keep dropping the ball in the relationship ? Maybe they aren't the best communicators, or there seems to be a lack of attention to your "love language" needs. It usually feels like pulling teeth, or just constant friction.

Sometimes for you, it's simply a lack of attention or a need for connection (Humans need connection so don't feel guilty to admit that yourself).

The attention we often seek is because we are diverting attention away from something we don't want to deal with (your past) but instead of guilting away from it how about you give into it. You don't ignore red lights.

"TELL ME ABOUT YOURSELF" THE EMOTIONAL RESUME.

* when we demand or expect that someone should treat us better than we treat ourselves, in that very moment we've missed the point.

* Treating yourself better means walking away from lopsided relationships.

* Treating yourself better also looks like you taking better care of how you show up. Sometimes our loyalty to someone else is betrayal to yourself and you are teaching (or continuing to teach) yourself "this is what I deserve".

The Work

There's a relationship you probably have right now where you're slightly miffed, and although it's dealing with the other person they probably have no idea.

Before you decide to talk to them about it, talk to yourself about it first because it may be a responsibility of your own that you're handing to someone else to deal with.

"What needs do I have right now that are not being met ?"

Just start there... and sit still enough to get the answer.

Try out this business model:

"What" What do I need from my relationships?

"Why?" Why are these things important to me ?

If it is attention... are you able to do something for yourself at this moment?

Well you're taking time to read this, so you're doing something for yourself and that's a start.

Leave your phone and go for a walk ... or take your phone just don't look at it for a while and allow your thoughts to come and go.

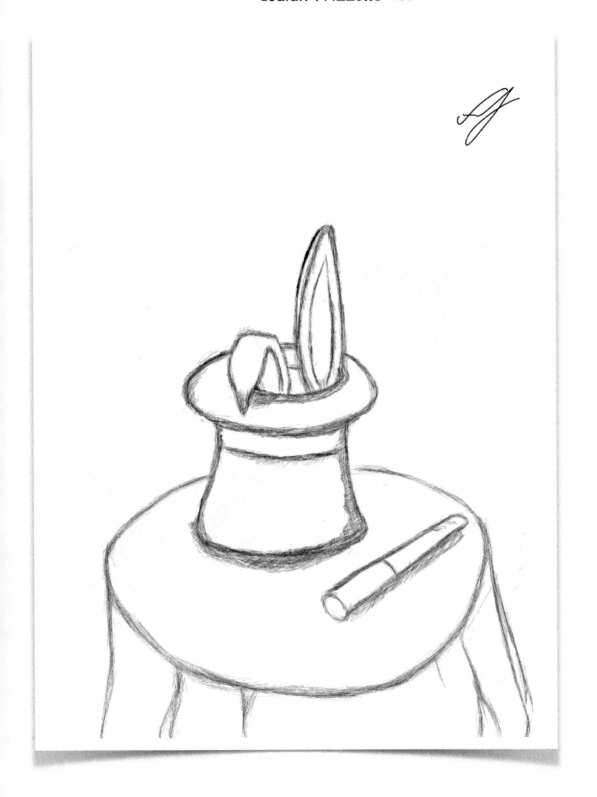

"Trigger Happy"

EMOTIONAL INTELLIGENCE

Humans are not robots, we have buttons (beyond just our belly buttons because those don't work for anything).

We're not always aware of what our buttons are, or why they exist until we are coming off the moment that triggered them.

If we are not aware of ourselves, it makes it entertaining/easier/scarier/confusing for others who experience us.

Self awareness requires you being honest with yourself when you are, and when you are not "you". The latter is the part that you hide away/ reject. How you respond when you are feeling hurt, angry, dejected are all important components of you, but also knowing the "why ?"

Vulnerability...It feels disgusting sometimes.

Vulnerability is better for you than it feels. Think of it like drinking a full glass of vegetables literally from the ground; It's healthier than it tastes, and there may be some particles in there that just don't sit right.

The reason why vulnerability feels so weird, is because it forces us to remove the veil, cut through the bullshit and face the parts of us that we stuff behind the clothes in our closet we haven't worn in years.

If you can dissect the reasoning behind the feelings, then you have a more objective approach to your behavior and in response, can be a little more patient with yourself.

I listened to a sermon recently about "offend-ability". Long story short, the easier you are offended, the higher your offend-ability, the lower your spirituality and in consequence the lower your emotional intelligence.

You can't tell me anything new about myself if I've already done the work to know myself...
You know that thing that gets to you?

It's something your parents, spouse, friend or relative has said or done to you over some time. Their awareness of your relationship with the offense makes the hit potent. They're seeking a specific response so they push the red button. You react as expected.

While you know what you are sensitive about , you have to look a little deeper at why it offends you at all. Once you look at that wound with some patience and with the intent to disinfect it, you can get past the initial disgust or pain. Objectify the offense. Take the burden off of you.

Blindspots though...
Something more insidious than being aware of what triggers you and preparing for the hit, is to not be aware !

Blindspots are those things that creep up that either we thought we were over, or something we are completely oblivious to !
 A blindspot feels like an attack from something harmless. The person didn't realize it'd affect you, shit you didn't realize it either.

"How are you when you don't get your way?"

Emotional intelligence will force you to take a look at the little kid in you, when they're left unattended. You know how children throw fits of rage when they don't get what they want or need ? Place that reaction in an emotionally stunted adult and you have some trouble. Sometimes, we become passive aggressive when we are upset that things didn't go our way. Other times we can just be mean, or maybe we resort to some self damage. Each of these responses are important to understand and recognize when you don't get your way because it points to your needs not being met and how someone in your life taught you to respond.

The Work

Think of something that really gets to you, I'm sure you have a storage space full of things, but for now just pick one.

It can be an insecurity.

A fear of being left out or ignored.

Something someone said recently

Sit there and ask yourself "why?" a couple of times, and each time you ask why, go deeper. In this exercise we are searching for the root cause, and the more you ask why the deeper your thinking travels in search of what's actually taking place.

By the end you should have the real reason.

Take your time with this one because it's a full glass of dirty earth veggies.

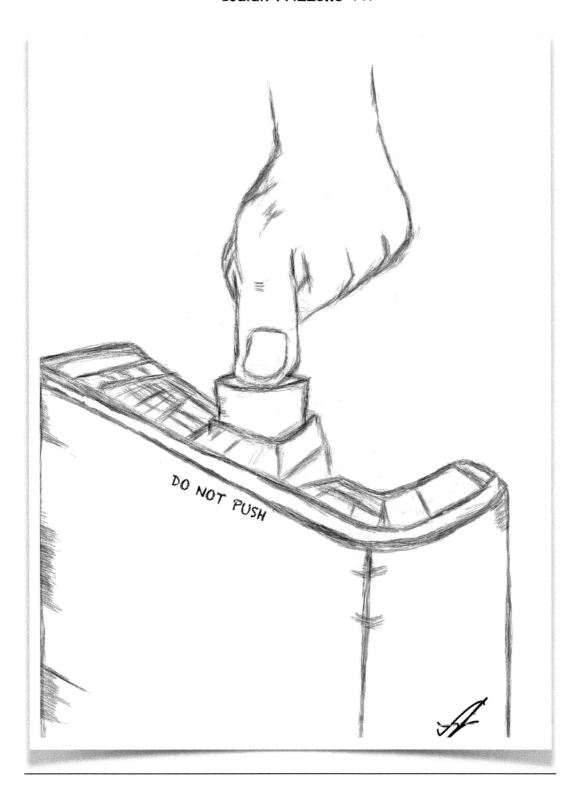

"That's not your bag"

"UM EXCUSE ME, YOU HAVE THE WRONG BAG"

You're at the airport waiting for your bag to fall from grace. you see it, grab for it, and B-line for the exit. Then, suddenly you're approached by someone telling you that's their bag. You could've sworn it was yours. It looks like it, feels like, but they're right, you got the wrong bag! At the moment you're alarmed, but then you laugh it off because, whoopsie-poopsie!

We carry around a lot of "bags" throughout our lives, don't we ? Sometimes we can confuse our bags with someone else's. We carry them, we stuff them with things (mine is full of chapstick and maybe Oreos) we think we need. We carry around baggage full of trauma as well, but I can almost promise you, there are a few bags that look like yours, but are certainly not.

You can be made to feel responsible for someone else's past experiences. They directly or indirectly demand you be their resolve from all they've experienced. If you are too young to understand or too oblivious, you eventually task yourself with a job that you will never be qualified for.

When you, or someone lashes out, in the moment there are things said that have nothing to do with the other person. Even your trajectory has nothing to do with the moment, instead past experiences. This process can either seem convoluted or very simple depending on your posture in the situation.

A good telltale sign of carrying someone else's "stuff" is feeling guilty without fully understanding why. You could be used to taking the hit for someone else's plight so automatically that's how you respond.

Or if you're the perp, saying things that you regret and understanding how hurtful and out of place they were. In the heat of the moment you think you are stating your case and saying things that need to be said, but nope, nope, nopity, nope, it was your trauma.

My friend coined the phrase, "I'm sorry that's just my trauma, put that down, that's not yours."

It's almost a miracle when someone (soon to be you) can recognize they are projecting their baggage onto someone or they've been lugging around bags that don't belong to them anymore -or ever. If we aren't careful, our identity is created from our trauma. If we are not careful we can walk through life identifying with it.

For a while it took me to learn that it wasn't me being an unhappy person, I just had projections on me creating that perception for me from someone else's unhappiness.

A lot of what you are carrying you don't need anymore... The weight just feels familiar and comfortable so you continue to carry it.

The work

It'll be easier to understand in practice.

The next time you feel like you are desiring something from someone, or they are seeking something from you, pause.

If you feel a familiar emotional response to someone who is fairly new in your life, pause.

The feeling will be very visceral. There will be a desire to pull away or lash out, either response is fear based.

Take a step back and ask yourself, "is this a trauma response?".

Look at the patterns of your relationships and see if you can find some similar moments.

Put one bag down at a time.

"Speak easy"

You have a voice right ? It's yours, not someone else's, use it !

This is a tough one because speaking up about things is not always the easiest. We run a script in our heads of the outcome before we say a word.

It's a fear that if you say what you feel you may lose a relationship, or you may be perceived in a certain way.

Here's something I've learned, and I mentioned it in an earlier chapter, no one who truly cares about you wants to know that you are suffering in silence at their hands or someone else's. We don't lose relationships, we learn what they actually look like. Saying what's on your mind/ heart (constructively) is not going to make someone who truly cares about you walk away. And if they do walk away then that's great! You're now fully aware of someone who didn't plan on taking care of your needs and were simply in your life for their own. Wish them well and redirect your focus.

But speaking your truth isn't always literally speaking, it can be you showing up as your most authentic self without an apology. Who you are, at your best, and worst but at your core 100% you, is your truth.

We all worry if people will like us but the most important is " do I even like me?. Have I taken the time to get to know myself."

Before we give someone the awesomeness that is us, we have to recognize the awesomeness that is us.

Yea you have flaws, that makes you, you.

Shitty past ? Ok cool you have an opportunity to make an awesome future starting with your present - because you're a gift.

Do you feel like you have qualities or parts of yourself to work on? Perfect! You recognize and see yourself, now you do the work to improve.

What I love about my relationships is that the people I have and hold dearest, all have backstory, all have done (or currently doing) the work to be some of the most beautiful people I know. Because of that, I love them even more.

If you take a good look at yourself you'll recognize you are that for someone else, and if not, be it for yourself and let that create space for the relationships to inevitably come.

Be willing to take up space in the world. Let people feel your weight when something is not okay with you.

You belong here just was much as anyone and should not be willing to endure anything you would not subject someone to.

You may not want to hurt or betray others and decide to keep quiet, but in that, you betray yourself by letting them subject you to it.

The Work

It's simple but super effective. Remind yourself today that you are loved, remind yourself that you don't deserve to endure mistreatment for the sake of maintaining a relationship. Remind yourself that anyone who values you wants to know you are well taken care of by them. Speak up when you feel slighted.

Take up space in a room that you've worked to be in. Be confident in who you are and who you've worked to be.

That's all...

COLOR CORRECTION

"Let's play detective"

THE BREAK UP

Something fell apart recently, or at some point things in life broke, or you yourself were in pieces because of it. I'll use a break up and you can insert what fits for you; trust me it'll make sense either way.

So something broke; that relationship, that job, that "thing". It was important to you and it weighed (weighs) on your head and heart. While you may have seen the situation from only your perspective and responsibility, there may have been more at play.

I went through a break up that had its impact on me. I was fully aware of the fact I did nothing short of my best and they admitted the same... so why did I still feel guilty? Every time I returned to the crime scene there was no evidence of my wrong doing, but that didn't stop me from subconsciously accusing myself for things going wrong. I should've been a surgeon because I can be pretty deadly with a metaphorical knife. Incision after incision I cut into layers of me to try to figure out what was wrong with me that made everything go wrong.

I showed compassion for the other person even though their actions were the direct causation of things ending, but you wouldn't know that.

"It's not you, it's me".

It can be hard to separate your accountability from someone else's responsibility if you were never in a position to feel validated.

You can make the mistake of blaming your existence for someone's reason to mistreat you... but you're not that special.

You deserve to be treated with kindness, respect, sincerity, and care like everyone else... But we don't always buy into that do we ?

I must warn you that this will not be a one quick fix, this just brings awareness to the fact that your self perception (love, esteem, worth) needs some fine tuning and will require you to do some deeper work, even therapy.

If you have people pleasing tendencies, you protect your offender and persecute your younger you. You attempt to pacify their wrong doing (enabling) while telling yourself in so many ways " It's not that big of a deal, you had to do something, you're always doing something wrong for this to keep happening". The truth is, you are doing something wrong, and that's believing that there is something inherently wrong with you.

Let's flip that.

Have you ever thought, "I gravitate towards relationships that reinforce a self limiting belief system because I feel most comfortable in that exchange" ? As painful as it may be (this recent situation was super painful) you engage and exist, even though it leaves you tearing away at parts of you.

When things fall apart, objectivity is paramount, otherwise you literally lose yourself. You think so much of yourself that you really think that someone's actions are a direct reflection of you ?... don't flatter

(flatten) yourself. It's tough, but it's VITAL to take small steps to recognize that someone's behavior is a reflection of their past experiences before you. They have history that you are not privy to,

YOU have history they are not privy to and the both of you show up with that information and do your dance.

I just want to let you know, if you are reading this book, you are someone of quality and honor; not because you are reading this book but because you are choosing to learn, grow, and heal...YOU ARE HUMAN.

Someone who makes the active choice to be better and do the work is someone who chose to deviate from things they may have endured, and by default that is a person that doesn't deserve to be mistreated by others, especially themselves. The other party needs healing too but it wasn't your job to fix the pieces.

The Work

"I deserve to be treated well, by myself and others".

"I deserve love."

"Even if I don't always believe it to be true, I am an amazing person and I am loved by others".

"It is not my job to fix others, I didn't break them, it is my responsibility to treat them well".

"The only thing wrong with me is that I think something is wrong with me."

Write it, say it in the mirror, when those other thoughts creep up, say them... DO THINGS TO REINFORCE Them!

"No Trespassing"

THE NECESSITY AND NUANCE OF BOUNDARIES.

When you hear the word "**boundary**" what do you think of first ?

I just pictured myself putting up a see through screen of some sort... Followed by an actual wall because sometimes a little piggy needs stronger material.

It's no surprise I struggled to sit down and write this chapter... I said to myself, "I don't know what to write" (and my nose grew a little).

Before you read on I want you to understand what boundaries are and who they are for.

Boundaries are for you; They help you to establish and recognize your level of value, worth, love, and respect. Boundaries keep you mentally, physically, and emotionally healthy, it also helps the other person. Keep that in mind moving forward. Say it in your head when you're in a moment that requires a boundary. When they're first implemented it will feel weird, why? Because you're not used to having any.

Personally, my learning of boundaries came from a lot of trial(s) and error. I'll use a few scenarios/ personal experiences to make it clear

That phrase "anything for family" is such a dangerous narrative. In some arenas, children grow into adults that feel obligated and indebted to very toxic relationships with their family members; siblings, extended relatives and most of all parents. There's a fear that if you don't do what this person asks, there will be dire consequences; A stripping of possessions, exile, inflicted harm or all the above.

The thought of going against a parent is absurd, regardless of what they may do to us. If you're reading this you're probably in your 20's or older and I'm here to tell you, AT NO AGE DO YOU DESERVE TO BE MISTREATED IN EXCHANGE FOR APPROVAL, ACCEPTANCE, OR LOVE. A healthy relationship has no daggers looming or strings tightly wound.

Start by saying "no". Sounds like such a piece of crap but start there. It's not easy, and there could be consequences but remind yourself, you are deserving of being treated just as well as this person demands you treat them.

If there's something that you don't feel comfortable doing, say "no". If there is a conversation you don't want to have that will affect you in some way make it clear you're not comfortable discussing the matter.

If you're older and you no longer live near your family, there could be a state of emergency every time the phone rings, and you're expected to fix it. Take your time answering the call or don't answer at all. I know it sounds shitty but trust me, take care of yourself. You are not obligated to be someone's dump. I've learned that in many cases there is not much I can do to help the issue and if it's just going to cause me an unhealthy amount of stress, I'm allowed to forfeit, but also it will give this person the opportunity to figure it out themselves or understand that I am not their life line anymore.

I will say for sure this is easier said than done, and sometimes you may need the help of external parties and that's okay, the goal here is to take care of your sense of self. That is top priority. I can't tell you how many times I felt like I was betraying or hurting someone by saying no. The guilt trip was all expense (my expense) paid and the mental damage leaves it's mark.

If you have this kind of dynamic in your familial relationships, you will grow to become a people pleaser and martyr in your relationships moving forward... How could I possibly know that, you say ? Call it a hunch.

OVEREXTENDING /PEOPLE PLEASING RELATIONSHIPS

Do you always make sure you're the friend/person someone can depend on ? If they needed to talk, needed help moving, a project, anything that required giving time and resources regardless of what you have going on. I'd rationalize a lot of times not getting my own things done to make sure I helped and sometimes it'd cost me, literally.

For example:

As a personal trainer I've learned that it takes a lot for people to sign on a dotted line and commit. Some people hate exercising, others don't want to necessarily pay for it. *Business and friendship is very dangerous when boundaries are not in place.

I had a friend that wanted to train with me.

I'd say at least 6 months passed of us working out together and I decided to propose to them becoming a paying client. In passing, they were all for it, but when it came time to attach commitment and compensation to it, she folded.

What that told me in the moment: My time, value, was not respected, it was just relied on because it was accessible.

I recognized I needed to set a boundary. At first I distanced myself and processed what I needed to.

I stopped making it a point to exercise with them. I told them I could no longer continue to train with them for free because this is my vocation. It felt weird. I felt like shit telling someone I was worth more than what they were offering me. Time had passed, and since we were friends there were other instances where I felt there was a "taking advantage of" being implemented, so I created space in communication. The end result is I felt better (still) and that was the most important, and maybe they understood the importance of valuing relationships a little more and respecting time. Our friendship was definitely compromised but what is a friendship that only one person is working to sustain properly ? My over-giving and over-extending was not healthy for the relationship.

Or what about being the reliable dependable friend/person for someone who isn't reciprocating because they don't feel the need to or see you as a friend on their end ?

You could easily say " that's not a good friend, you should've just walked away." You're not wrong, but let us go back to our original topic about feeling obligated to relationships no matter how much you're mistreated because you feel indebted despite what you receive. On top of that, if you truly care about people, you will not readily turn on your heels.

Only recently, did I make it a point to be there more for myself than them. I'm a person and I care about myself so it's about time I start acting like it. If the relationship was on their terms then there would be no need to change.

I've found myself over-giving because I felt like I was obligated and my worth was tied up in how much I was able to endure. Saying no made me a "bad person" or someone they wouldn't want to be around any longer. On my end I never knew what to expect from those relationships because they operated on their terms.

I didn't consider how much of an emotional and mental toll it was taking on me, and on top of everything, life has definitely been an uphill journey if it hasn't been clear yet.

How often are you the "go-to" for everyone's heavy load ?

You get a bunch of missed calls from a friend or family member. They had the "worst day of their life", or they just went through something, or they need your advice. You've probably had a run of the mill day yourself or maybe it was solid and you're feeling great, but after their grievances have been aired out and your head's spin cycle is finished they tell you that they have to go. *call ended*

or

There seems to be someone in your life that is perpetually toxic or feels the need to negatively critique your every move through life.

or

Maybe there's just that someone who is not the kindest to you or never cares to see how you're doing...

You know that person that is notoriously late, or isn't as responsive as they demand others be for them. If it doesn't make you feel good why do you keep showing up for it? Do you treat them that way or have you been consistent and reliable ? I didn't say perfect, I said consistent.

As much as society talks about the importance of chemistry when finding your significant other, you think it'd be a heavier emphasis on the need for boundaries because that is also a chemistry.

If you're a fixer, you're probably a people pleaser, which means that you likely have little to no boundaries and have no idea what they are.

MOURNING RELATIONSHIPS

Setting boundaries will have casualties.

It may feel unnatural but it's necessary and I cannot stress that enough. I've come to understand I cultivated plenty of imbalanced relationships because I lacked self love and in turn, lacked boundaries that would let me know that I deserve better. I've felt much better since then. Some conversations I made a point to have about how I felt and others I simply let time itself be the executioner.

What I've understood in all of these situations is that if someone walks away because I implemented a boundary, then that means they were benefiting from me having none. You're better off. You have to be willing to cut the cords of relationships that are draining you of your peace. It will hurt, but just because you're used to enduring a certain level of treatment does not mean you deserve to continue.

No one who benefits from your lack of self care will ever tell you to care more about yourself if it compromises their incentives.

I got in the habit of saying "it's all good". It's not. If it doesn't make you feel good then stop continuing to endure it.

The Work

Start recognizing how you feel in exchanges within your relationships. My barometer is an underlying feeling of fear, guilt, or resentment.

Be patient and compassionate with yourself as you notice those feelings, they're just indicating the parts needing some care. Like a wall, when something feels imbalanced there needs to be a boundary brick in place... But we're not here to build walls if we don't have to... just parameters.

You deserve what you are willing to give.

" That's your power "

We are all hiding parts of ourselves from the rest of the world out of fear it will push them away.

Picture this: A family is in a car and they've just pulled up to someone's house or a function and the parents turn to the kid, " Don't do that thing that you do". Sometimes it is necessary to remind your children to be on their best behavior, but what about when you are reminding your child to not express themselves or be themselves to appease the masses ?

Fast forward to adulthood.

We become those parents to ourselves.

Ever have one (or many) of those moments through life you shamed yourself for being sensitive or caring? Or there's this quirk of yours that you kick yourself for having.

Maybe you're hyper sensitive, you're a sucker for sentiments, or you pay attention to the little things more than most. What about the way you organize (My shirts are in the order of hues).

You are probably really good with numbers or your ability to correlate polar opposites to one another to make sense is odd but always plausible... We all have different super powers.

Ready for this...

The thing(s) about yourself that you try to push down or are ashamed to share, is the very thing that makes you so much of you; FYI there are people that experience it and love you for it.

So how about you be one of those people ?

We down play our ability to affect those around us just by existing. The beauty in that is when we are being ourselves, that is the very thing that someone else may need.

In the previous chapters I talked about the necessity of boundaries or being the "go to", but in a healthy exchange, you never know how much it means for someone to be on the receptive end of a good listener without judgement.

To recognize your power, you have to recognize those moments you shame yourself. You gave someone a gift and it seems like they may have not appreciated it ? Embarrassment sets in. You call yourself stupid for even considering it. You just turned to your child in the back seat and shamed them.

The flip side is this, you were thinking of someone without them realizing and you extended that to them. You're thoughtful without prompt, honor that. It's our ability of innocence that needs to be appreciated.

We learn shame from a young age. We learn the need to wear faces to exist in our experiences.

The gesture wasn't reciprocated or appreciated and you feel defective. Contrary to the rhetoric, vulnerability is one of the strongest things you can be capable of. Vulnerability requires honesty, with ourselves and others, and honesty feels weird when we are not used to it. What I've come to understand is that vulnerability, and sincerity will only distance the people who are not a reflection of those things and strengthen the bond with the ones who are.

Be weird, and by weird, I mean be you. I'm not saying hide in someone's bushes or throw rocks at someone's window at midnight (because that's called being invasive and overstepping boundaries) I'm saying to live in the parts of you that you fear expressing.

Lean in to your process, it's worth it. Validate your pain, you're worth it. That "it's all good" cuts off your power circuit. "If I know what is happening in me I can make things happen through me."

In your weakest moments will you find what you are truly capable of, mentally, emotionally, physically, spiritually.

That's my gift to you, confirmation that being open breeds opportunity, not always in material, but mental and emotional peace. The more you are open to looking at, the more you are able to heal from.

The Work

Moving forward, in those moments of fear of expressing yourself, you will lean into it more with a smile. I'm not saying change the world overnight, because the thought of that just stressed ME out. The moment you feel shame for your sensitivity, say "thank you instead". The moment you think of someone beyond yourself say " I appreciate you for being this way." That quirk of yours, " This makes me so damn dope."

"The Lord always helps the dreams of people thinking about other people."

" Did you eat ? "

A LOVE LANGUAGE

Growing up my mom always had this thing of "text me" or "call me when you get there". Once I got older, and lived on my own it became "text me when you get home."

When I was younger I assumed it was a check in process, but because of my mom's line of work, I learned to appreciate it more. There were some nights she'd get home later than usual, but I remember one night in particular seemed a little out of the ordinary. I later found out that she did in fact get caught up in a dangerous exchange.

We all know tomorrow isn't promised, but we navigate our relationships like it's guaranteed. And saying "I love you" can feel trite if it's just a phrase more than an actual feeling behind it. There are so many more ways to show and say it though. If you get the chance, check out "5 love languages" and thank me later.

As I've gone through life, I've taken that practice with the people in my life. Sometimes saying "hey I love you" mid convo seems out of whack but, "How was your day?", "Did you eat ?" carries weight.

"It's not about the words"(my acting teacher always emphasized that).

We give words meaning, subtext, and feeling, but our intention is everything. See, the person may not realize it but, by asking those kinds of questions, you're finding other ways to say " Hey, I love you and your well being is a priority to me."

Also a great way to know how much someone means to you, think about when you have good news ... who are the people you want to share that with?

Sometimes it may just be something funny in the day that happened, who are the people you want to share that with ?

As people, our goal is to connect to "home". Home is not always a place, it can be a person, or even an object. Our actions in our relationships indicate how much we feel at home with others.

"Did you make it home ok?"

Some people say, "Well what if I didn't make it home there's nothing you can technically do about it." Yea they're right, but we attend funerals and express how much we love someone when they've passed on right ? So what's the harm in doing that now? You will never hear someone complain about being important to someone (in a healthy way), because as people we want to matter.

When someone that has investment in your life says they're proud of you how does that make you feel ?

Detach fear, guilt, and rejection, from affection. We fear that by showing people we care we run the risk of losing them, but you can never lose something when you are showing genuine value and gratitude.

The Work

If you're not the type of person that says I love you, or you cringe when you hear it and people around you know that, listen to the other things they may be saying instead, and try saying the aforementioned phrases yourself.

If you are one of those people that says "I love you" without pause, and think that it may not land, try just checking in.

Or just continue doing what you do cause, "Ain't nothing like the real thing baby".

It's not about the words, it's about letting people know they matter to us in so many words.

"Connection is currency"

INVESTMENTS VS. INCENTIVES

True friendship is probably one of life's most priceless, and undervalued things. I'm a sucker for it. I believe we all are. Our approach as individuals can vary because not everyone defines friendship the same, but we can all agree that it's precious. "It's about the people you want to share your favorite things with; For me it's desserts (DONT JUDGE ME!) because it's an opportunity to connect and share space.

So how do you discern a true friendship from an "incentive exchange" though ?

"The best way to find a friend is to be one."

INCENTIVES

There are instances throughout life that connections are labeled as friendships, but may not be. I like to define those as incentives. Incentives represent an investment made because there's a payoff. I mean the goal in friendship is to connect and build a relationship, so that could be considered an incentive, but what I'm referring to is a little more superficial than that.

" Yea they are my friend. I get access to a bunch of spots and they know a ton of people that I can network with."

"Do you guys hang out ?"

"Not unless there's an event. Or we see each other at a gathering."

"I'm only friends with Isaiah because I need that damn cake recipe and once I get it I'm OUT!" * And scene*

That's a pretty Hollywood example, but I'm sure you've either been on one end of this exchange or heard it verbatim...

But also, over my body will someone get that cake recipe from me!

Do you have that friend that only reaches out when they are in need, but they never make a point to make plans or see how you are ?

" When the chips fall, who you gonna call ?"

There's an incentive there, you are their lifeline but only that.

INVESTMENTS

" I feel like I can trust them with everything honestly, I don't feel judged. We check in with one another. We do a bunch of things together, they don't hesitate to call me on my bs, and at the same time encourage me to do better. We hold each other accountable."

*Friendship requires intimacy: Trust, reciprocation, effort, acceptance, forgiveness, accountability, nurture, love, patience, support, and the willingness to understand one another when there are differences more than the knee-jerk need to be right.

The last part can be tough since we are all carrying some history of life. What comes off as needing to be right and in control is truly just a need to be understood, valued and acknowledged... Please remember that, especially when it comes to the people you really love.

So friendship...

It's A SHIP, people ! True relationships require moving and functional parts to be sustained properly orrrr they sink.

As we get older it's important to understand the kind of friends we have, want, and are. The purpose or need that a friendship serves in your life at any point can always change, but you'll only be aware of it if you're aware of yourself.

Like any investment It's important to give friendships room to grow, closer or apart. Do not be afraid of change, because without change there is no growth. I'll repeat, Do not be afraid of change, because without change, there is no growth.

Maybe there's a change in the air, and you feel it. You and your buddy went from talking daily to every now and then. It can hurt for sure, because you feel like you are drifting apart. Sometimes that's not the case. Sometimes there is just a shedding of what your relationship was. What was required in that season to establish one another is no longer necessary.

It's weird but you want your friends to be okay... near or far, even if you may not be on the best terms, in your heart of hearts you want them to be well taken care of. You want to connect. Maybe not all the time but you still want to be a part of each other's lives just because... that's the key.

The "Just because".

I'm not seeking anything from you and you're not seeking anything from me, we just value the space we have and take up in one another's life.

Maybe there is a relationship that went sour, and maybe it doesn't feel like they were much of a friend... But for your sanity and peace, can you recognize and accept that at one point in time there may have been a necessary connection ?

Relationships are lessons, blessings, seasons, and reasons.

Sometimes we may not have the most healthy friendships. They feel toxic and or obligatory. There's more pressure than pleasure to maintain the friendship.

IT'S A LESSON

You hesitate to share good news with a friend because they may not be happy for you. Sometimes you're the friend to them more than they are to you. It's still an investment, the interest is a little skewed though.

What are the feelings or thoughts that come to mind when you think of some of your connections ?

Do you have to mentally prepare yourself to spend time with some people versus the day going too fast when you are with them ?

With Some friendships you may be holding on to, does the person only appear to take?

Orrrr maybe you are all the things listed above!! If so it's all good, this is an opportunity to grow right ?

I̲T̲'̲S̲ ̲A̲ ̲S̲E̲A̲S̲O̲N̲

But there are friendships that grow apart, some having more specific reasons than others but when that does happen that can be an indication of a divergence of paths.

** I've learned that not every friendship swims in the same waters.

Now hear me out, I don't think it's emotionally and or mentally possible to have a bunch of friends at one point in your life if you're doing the dance properly. I do feel you can have friends at different stages though, and if you are lucky you will have a few that exist throughout each stage.

A friend of mine made sense of the different levels of friendship for me.

"Rings" as she described them have people at different levels and they all are representative of the level of intimacy. Yes, friendship requires a level of intimacy and reciprocation that wouldn't be necessary with strangers, but not all of them will exist in the same realm. And they shouldn't !! It's impossible to have 20 close friends and if you do, there is some work to be done.

Blessing

It's a blessing if the friends you have carry through your life with the through line being the two of you growing yet still coming back to center.

Connection is currency and it's vital to be fully aware of your connections.

But in any form there's always something to take away from it. The currency, the value of the relationship or the value of the lesson.

It's important that we understand relationships are or should be treated as a delicate piece of ourselves. I've learned through so many relationships the importance of that very thing.

Friendship is underrated, undervalued and in some cases treated passively, but friendship can be the family you found along your journey. Friendship done right can be the missing pieces. Friendship can be the breath of fresh air you've been seeking.

The work

When you think of friends, who all comes to mind first ?

Write them down and attach a word to them.

If you want to take it a step further, reach out to a friend that means a lot to you. Despite the time that has passed since you've last spoken, let them know how much they mean to you and that you value them. Don't expect or look for a response, just share that with them.

Where's that other shoe ?

" WAIT THINGS FEEL GOOD, SOMETHING IS WRONG"

Want to know something interesting ? Some people out there believe that if their relationship(s) doesn't have any drama/conflict, then that means something is wrong! I'm not saying relationships are supposed to be perfect, I'm saying that they don't always require discord to progress. When someone is uncomfortable with peace in their relationships, it's indicative that they find peace in chaos and turbulence and in actuality are not at peace at all.

It's learned, it's taught, it's experienced... Mix those three and it becomes your belief system. Your normal is actually abnormal. We are not meant to be in a constant state of fear or tension in our day to day.

I remember back in college, my friend and I at the time always became concerned if we were having consecutive good days. Too many good days in a row meant something bad was coming.

We were usually right.

But there is a way to create the environment for your desired outcome. You start looking for the problem... and you keep looking until you find it.

Are you the kind of person that looks at every little thing in a good situation with a magnifying glass because something just doesn't seem right ? I'm not saying don't trust your intuition when things feel off, I'm saying it's important to examine if you find a way to make every slight hiccup indicate that the entire situation is no good or "too good to be true".

We are taught not to enjoy our experiences and always prepare for the worst. We grow up in toxic and turbulent environments and believe that's how things should be because it's what we know.

But guess what ? You are wearing the other shoe that you're expecting to drop. It's all good. Just as we are taught to prepare for the worst when good things are happening, we deserve to prepare for the best when days are the stormiest.

We believe there's a catch to every situation if we believe that we don't deserve good things to happen for us.

"I fear success and love so I killed it before it had the chance to attack me."
When you are used to the other shoe phenomena you'll even steer clear
of success in profession and relationships because you're already
expecting them to fail. When they do fail you can say "I told you so".
But we don't always recognize we are molding the environment to work
in favor of our fears.

The work

Something is going well in your life ? It feels right ? Lean into that and say to yourself "I deserve this".

And if you're still unsure, say to yourself " I will be fine either way".

" I will survive "

HOW ABOUT YOU THRIVE INSTEAD ?

YOU ARE NOT YOUR BURDENS, or EXPERIENCES.

If there is anything you take from this, it is the importance of separating your trials from your truth.

What you focus on you fester.

I've gone through most of my life thinking and truly believing that I have to struggle ... "It's life that's just what it's going to be".

To some degree there is truth in that, but very little in comparison to what I created in my mind's world .

I'm not saying don't work for things.

I'm sure as hell not saying don't give your absolute best to attain the goals you seek. What I'm saying to you is,

You don't have to struggle in order to be loved.

You don't have to trench through mud and quicksand to be worthy of this life, and on top of that you don't have to be willing to take anything someone wants to give you instead of what you deserve. You can usually tell a person that was raised on love and peace and a person that was

raised in survival mode.

Nothing ever feels safe... and even safe spaces seem to have live mines just waiting. I've truly been that person. I am that person. Survival mode is the only mode I know for myself. It drives me bonkers but there are moments when I'm able to say to myself " You don't have to struggle" YOU DON'T DESERVE TO STRUGGLE.

It took me a while to get that and even still I have to make a conscientious effort to take myself out of survival mode when things happen.

First of all, shit happens... maybe more than often for some, but it's inevitable.

My experiences have made me feel like I'm probably one of the most undeserving, wicked people to walk this earth. Truly. There was no real evidence. I was too young to realize that although I was held responsible for a lot of things and other people's feelings, they weren't my responsibility. We all play a particular role in other people's lives. Records have shown I've always been the helper to some degree and eventually I started putting myself in that position for others just because It was what I was used to. I wanted to help of course but sometimes it went beyond that.

I'm no superhero, I'm a human being with pieces to me that may not all be there, so going into situations trying to fix someone else's broken with no reciprocation, left pieces of me feeling unwanted.

The "martyr" mentality at times leaves you the victim of your own scheming. Stop that. Oddly enough there is comfort in discomfort for some just because it's what they are used to. It's commonplace no matter how bad it may feel. Home for some was built on very shaky ground.

Think about this...

Are you holding the keys to the prison you built for yourself?

Kind of rhetorical but someone else or something else cannot release you from a prison that you yourself concocted and keep renovating.

You keep moving the keys (You keep moving the rabbit)
you keep extending your own sentence

The reason may change from time to time as well, but we are really creative without realizing it.

What happens when you say to yourself " I'm responsible for my own hardships and feelings of sorrow ".

Think about it. A situation of any kind, haunts us because we choose to replay it constantly. That's our doing. Yes maybe the situation wasn't the most ideal *insert person, place, or thing* and it left some very crazy feelings, but if you're still experiencing the pain from that situation and it's not currently happening to you now, then yes you're the perpetrator not them or that.

The Work

"I am not not my burdens, I deserve blessings."

"I do not have to be on empty to be filled."

" I matter and I am loved by those around me, and I work diligently to show myself that love in my habits, my relationships, my focus, my eating, and my words."

"Tough love"

"YOU'RE EASY TO LOVE"

Not sure how we got to a place in the world where the idea of being loved/valued without you having to sacrifice your sense of self or endure more than you should, is unfathomable... But we are here and parked!

Ya got ya road snacks? Good because we are leaving and are not making any stops so use the bathroom now.

If you are reading this, you are probably looking to improve your life in one way or another. You are looking to improve your relationships, change some habits, but underneath all of that is you wanting to appreciate yourself more.

Along your journey you may have felt or been taught that you, because of who you are just by existing, have to work extra hard to be appreciated and seen.

On a basic level we all are deserving of love and value.

As we journey through life we experience lopsided relationships, treatment, or scenarios that leave us confused about our actual worth when it comes to how other people see us.

There's a relationship in your life that was more of a dangling carrot. The dynamic in place was conditional love, "you're only as lovable as what you can offer in the moment, if you don't meet my needs, you're nothing to me".

Emotional abandonment is a real thing. This happens early on, and in process we constantly seek the need to be chosen in our adult lives.

Because of that we believe we are hard to love. You're not.

I'm telling you you're not and you know why ? because you probably go above and beyond. You show up, you do more than asked, you do your best to just treat others well and there may be a lack of reciprocation but you still show up.

Aside from anything you offer up, it's the fact that you are capable.

You don't have to go through rings of fire to be appreciated or cared for. The proof is in the people that are present in your life for good, bad, and indifferent. The moments you weren't at your best, who was around ? The parts of you that you deem unlovable, who are the people still currently in your life and want you around? Those people are all reminders that you don't have to work that hard or feign perfection to be preferred or sought after. The challenge is to stop seeking that validation from empty connections.

The Work

Moving forward I want you to be mindful of the relationships you're cultivating. Do they feel lopsided? notice that ... Do you feel like you're over giving yourself to receive approval ? Recognize it.

In all those moments I want you to say to yourself "I'm not hard to love and I don't have to work this hard for it." and in that very moment stop trying. Talk to someone you trust about it. Have that dialogue.

You are loved more than you think, trust me.

If you lean into the little things that people do without you asking, you will realize and understand how much they value you.

" I got this."

You've always had it.

So... we've reached the end... but also the beginning because life is a semicolon.

Have you revisited that first coloring page ?

What does it look like now? How have you treated it up until now ?

Has it changed at all ? When you look at it do you feel differently than you did the first time?

You may not feel different, but if you've been doing the work then things are not the same.

You have a community now. You've created a safer place for your feelings and thoughts, inside of you. Whatever or whoever you pray to... know that you are well taken care of. You got this because you got others. You got this because you got yourself.

When we do the work to start treating ourselves better, subconsciously we are telling ourselves that we are valued, we matter and despite how fearful of our feelings and insecurities we may be, we are still willing to push past that.

I thought I'd need my PhD before I wrote a book. For a while I thought the only way anyone would take me seriously is if I had an office and my degree hanging on my wall- but I've been doctoring and healing myself through experiences for quite some time. I don't need a degree to speak of my own story. Being human, and open can be the most potent medicine you will need to articulate a remedy for others.

So in a moment of doubt, despair, upheaval, discomfort, ambiguity, sadness, or even happiness, success, and elation remind yourself "I got this." In moments you may feel like you don't, look at all the moments you've already made it through to get to this very moment.

One of the most realistic and potent examples I can use is going for a run. It hurts, it's exhausting and sometimes it's "what the hell am I doing and why ?!" every time your foot hits the ground. But what I've trained myself to recognize while running is that every moment I've wanted to give up has already passed and I've gone further in the same moment that I wanted to stop. Does it hurt ? Well it was hurting 10 minutes ago and it still hurts but obviously I can take it. Your progress is still taking place in your moments of wanting to throw it all away.

What your external world is, is a reflection of the work you've been doing and you should be nothing but proud because YOU DID THE WORK.

And the work continues from here.

For the rest of your life you will be more aware of your triggers to some degree, more cognizant of your relationships with others and how they reflect on some parts of you that require healing and "re-parenting". Don't get hung up on getting it right every time because you're a human, full of colorful experiences that you've gradually accumulated over time.

We don't allow perfection here. We welcome persistence. Potency.

Patience...And most importantly love... for yourself first so you can properly pour it on thick to others.

Trust yourself a little more now, this is not a negotiation sir/mam. I don't care who you are, if you're trying to do better, I'm rooting for you so hard!

The Work

"Color".

You deserve it.

A VERY SPECIAL THANK YOU TO MY FAMILY AND THE FRIENDS WHO HAVE BECOME FAMILY...

THANK YOU FOR KEEPING MY GARDEN GREEN.

AND A VERY SPECIAL THANK YOU TO EACH AND EVERY PERSON WHO IS NOW WALKING AROUND WITH A NEW "PALETTE".

CPSIA information can be obtained
at www.ICGtesting.com
Printed in the USA
LVHW061629080522
718198LV00008B/434